THE CIRCUS

Written by

Catherine Wilkinson

Illustrated by

Angela Mingledorff

DEDICATION

Dedicated to my little man.

ABOUT THIS BOOK

These books are designed to be interesting for your child. I hope that they will find it interesting to learn about the different emotions and things that they can see in their world. With these books and also the SELIA Kids program, my aim is to promote an introduction to emotional, cognitive and environmental awareness. Research has shown that a foundation in awareness can lead to better choices, decision making and problem solving. And that these can lead to a more fulfilling life for the individual and the people around them. Part of the importance of learning these skills is the practice of slowing down to become aware of and acknowledge what is happening around us.

Often so much is happening in our lives and our children's lives that children can get over stimulated and overly involved in the situation without realising. The danger in this is that behaviours can happen that are not healthy, or sometimes not how we would usually have liked to have behaved ourselves or have had our children behave. When we become over stimulated and bombarded with information, be it social, environmental, relational, or emotional, we start to lose the opportunity to think and make decisions.

Critically we lose the opportunity to learn the skills we need to live healthy and fulfilling lives. Often we don't realise we do not have the right skills to use within the challenging situation until we really need them! This is exactly what these series of books are designed to do, to teach your child and open the communication lines to develop strong social and emotional skills. Skills such as resilience, confidence, teamwork, leadership, self discipline, delayed gratification, and emotional regulation.

You will find as you spend time with your child with these books, and implementing the techniques, that your relationship with your child will change. You will notice your own understanding is improved, your child is more responsive, and your relationship will be strengthened. The questions within the books are designed to promote conversation in general, but also to set a precedent of your child feeling comfortable in talking with you about their feelings from a very early stage where your relationship is the most important one in their life. Please use the questions as a prompt, though expand and add your own experiences to connect with your child where possible. I hope that you will enjoy them too!

Catherine Wilkinson

BA (Psych)(Hons), Dip Prof Couns, Cert Frontline Management, Cert 1 Trainer, ...and Mum!

One day a big bright red and yellow tent was standing right in the middle of the field near Aston's house.

Can you point to the tent? What else can you see there?

A new circus was in town, with camels and lamas, and beautiful white horses.

How many horses can you see? Count the horses together.

Aston thought the big circus tent looked like fun, and he wanted to go and see the animals. "Can we go and look mum, pleeeeease?", he asked.

Discuss why we speak politely with others.

"Okay", his mum said. So Aston's mum took him over to the field to get a closer look.

What animals can you see now? What else can you see? How do you think Aston is feeling walking over to see the animals?

Oh dear, but when they got a little closer, suddenly all the animals looked a lot bigger!

Look how much bigger the elephant is compared to Aston! Do you have a pet that is bigger or maybe even smaller than you? What do you like about that pet?

Aston felt afraid
of the big animals!

Can you see how Aston
looks afraid?

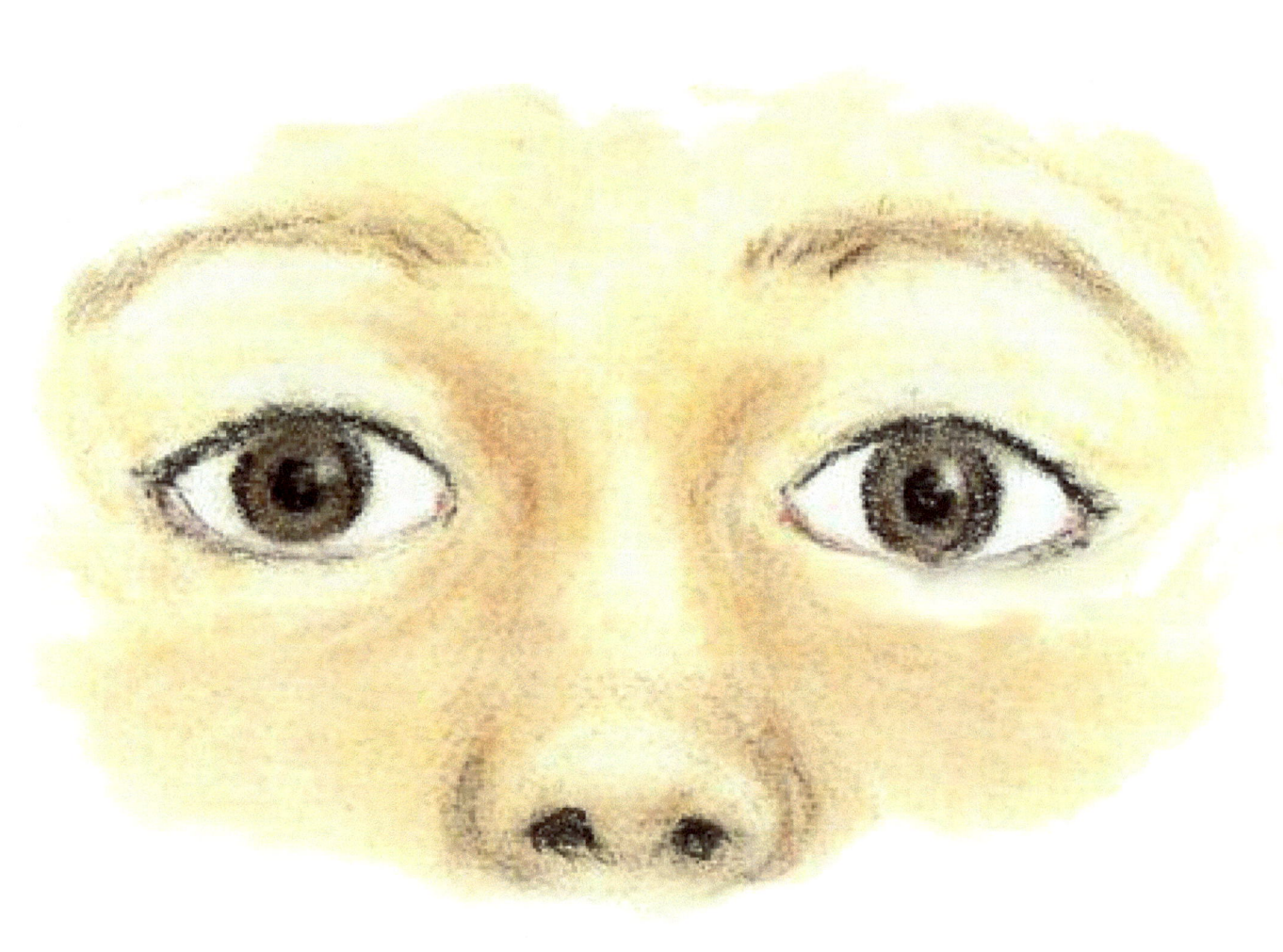

His eyes are very wide and his eyebrows are raised bunched together in the middle.

Point to them.

His head tilted back a little and his mouth is open so wide he took a big breath in.

Can you show me your afraid face?

Yes!
He was afraid alright!
"Pick me up"
he asked his mum.

Do you remember a time when maybe you felt afraid? What was happening? I remember I time I felt afraid too...

That made him feel a lot safer! He wasn't afraid anymore.

Can you see how Aston felt scared and so he asked his mum for help? What do you think you could do when you feel afraid? Brainstorm a few ideas.

SELIA KIDS PROGRAM

SELIA Kids is a division of the Social and Emotional Learning Institute Australia (SELIA). It is an opportunity for parents and carers to connect with their children and teach them the vital skills they need whilst growing in these critical stages of development and especially towards starting school. Skills for development that they will carry through into adolescence and adulthood.

The Social and Emotional Learning Institute Australia (SELIA) was founded to establish social and emotional learning (SEL) as a fundamental part of child education. We operate a multi faceted approach working with families with children from 0 to 6 years through our SELIA Kids program, and working with principals and leaders from primary schools throughout Australia. Our consultants and program developers work with advisors in the United States, the UK and New Zealand to ensure up to date and established SEL practices.

SELIA is *Putting the Pieces Together* for child academic, social, and emotional education.

Social and emotional learning (SEL) is a strategy for developing the essential life skills necessary for greater success throughout all the different aspects of life. SEL builds the skills we all need to manage our lives, our relationships, and our study or work, more effectively and with greater satisfaction. Skills such as recognising and managing our emotions, making responsible decisions, handling challenging situations constructively, and establishing fulfilling relationships.

In respect of children, these skills help them to understand what they are feeling and make appropriate behaviour response choices that further help them to keep themselves safe and resolve conflicts or confrontations more effectively.

The Collaborative for Social and Emotional Learning (CASEL) has identified five core groups of social and emotional competencies:

· *Self-awareness*—accurately assessing one's feelings, interests, values, and strengths; maintaining a well-grounded sense of self-confidence

· *Self-management*—regulating one's emotions to handle stress, control impulses, and persevere in overcoming obstacles; setting and monitoring progress toward personal and academic goals; expressing emotions appropriately

· *Social awareness*—being able to take the perspective of and empathize with others; recognizing and appreciating individual and group similarities and differences; recognizing and using family, school, and community resources

· *Relationship skills*—establishing and maintaining healthy and rewarding relationships based on cooperation; resisting inappropriate social pressure; preventing, managing, and resolving interpersonal conflict; seeking help when needed

· *Responsible decision-making*—making decisions based on consideration of ethical standards, safety concerns, appropriate social norms, respect for others, and likely consequences of various actions; applying decision-making skills to academic and social situations; contributing to the well-being of one's school and community

Please visit our website at www.seliakids.com.au

or for primary school educators www.selinstituteaustralia.com.au